THE BATTLE OF MARATHON

Contents

Steck
Vaughn™

A Harcourt Achieve Imprint

www.Steck-Vaughn.com
1-800-531-5015

How far would you go to help your friends and family? This book is about a teenager in ancient Greece. He went to great lengths for his city. He literally ran hundreds of miles!

My name is Herodotus (huh-*rod*-uh-tus). I was born in Greece thousands of years ago. History was my favorite subject. The Battle of Marathon was my favorite story.

As I tell you more, remember these facts.

Big Ideas

- The empire of Persia stretched from modern-day Turkey to India. One of its great rulers was Darius. The homeland of the Persians is now called Iran.

- Darius tried to conquer the areas along the Mediterranean Sea.

- Greek civilization was based on the city-state. Independent cities elected their own leaders. Our own government is modeled on some ideas from the city of Athens.

- The ancient Greeks held a sports event every four years at Mount Olympus. The modern Olympics are based on these games.

After I grew up, I wrote books about Greek history, especially the wars. If you wrote about your country, what things would you include?

The Battle of Marathon was very important. The Persians attacked Athens. A young messenger was asked to help save his city. The words below will help you follow his story.

Vocabulary

conquer to defeat an enemy; to take over a place by force

*The Persian king wanted to **conquer** Greece.*

---

forum a public place where debates are held

*A student council meeting is a good **forum** for discussing school rules.*

---

opposition a group or attitude that fights against another group or idea

*Our team faced tough **opposition** in the tournament.*

---

sequence a set of things in a particular order

*A strange **sequence** of events led to the crash.*

---

tactic a method or plan used to achieve a goal

*Our main **tactic** was to pass the ball a lot.*

Characters

Phidippides
(fi-*dip*-uh-dees),
an Athenian runner
and soldier

Callimachus
(cal-*lim*-uh-kus),
the Athenian
commander

Miltiades
(mil-*tee*-u-dees),
an Athenian general

Themistocles
(thuh-*mis*-tuh-kleez),
an Athenian officer

Aeschylus
(*es*-ki-lus),
an Athenian soldier
and playwright

Hegesipyle
(hegg-eh-*sip*-i-lee),
wife of Miltiades

Darius,
Emperor of Persia

In 499 B.C., the Greeks in Ionia rebelled against their Persian rulers. The city of Athens sent ships and soldiers to help the Ionians. The fighting lasted five years.

GREECE

Sparta→

Athens

Ionia

PERSIAN EMPIRE

Persepolis

In the end, the Persian ruler, Darius, *defeated* the Ionians. He never forgave Athens.

The Athenians will feel the *might* of the Persian empire! We will *conquer* Athens itself!

In 490 B.C., Darius sent an army to attack Athens. They landed at Marathon.

Run to Athens! Tell them the Persian army has arrived!

The Athenians debated about what they should do. The agora, or marketplace, was their forum for political discussions.

I bring news! The Persian army has landed at Marathon!

We can't wait for the Persians to attack. We must attack them first!

But there are over 25,000 Persian soldiers. We only have 9,000 men!

A young soldier named Aeschylus watched closely. He would become a great **playwright** and write many dramas about war.

Phidippides, have you heard? The Persian army is coming!

We must help defend Athens!

Vote with me! Who's for marching our soldiers to Marathon?

On to Marathon!

Let's fight!

Find me the best runner in Athens. I have an important *mission* for him.

Phidippides is our fastest messenger.

Run to Sparta immediately. If we are to defeat the Persians, we will need support from their army.

I won't let Athens down, sir!

7

The Athenian troops marched to Marathon to meet the enemy.

No matter how tired I get, I must keep going!

At the same time, Phidippides set out for the city of Sparta. The journey was nearly 150 miles. Much of it was over rough *terrain*.

After about 36 hours of running, Phidippides arrived in Sparta.

8

So you see, that's why Athens needs your help.

We will send troops soon. But our soldiers are not allowed to fight until the next full moon.

But sir, that's several days away!

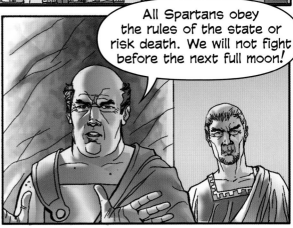

All Spartans obey the rules of the state or risk death. We will not fight before the next full moon!

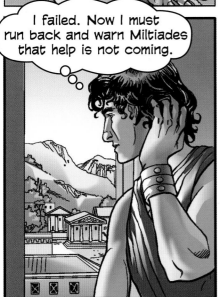

I failed. Now I must run back and warn Miltiades that help is not coming.

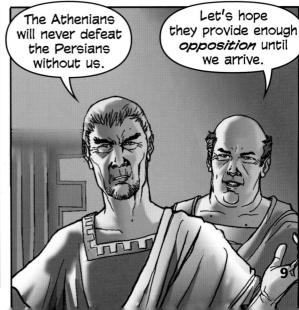

The Athenians will never defeat the Persians without us.

Let's hope they provide enough *opposition* until we arrive.

9

Themistocles, you were right. We are outnumbered at least three-to-one.

Miltiades is coming. He will lead us to victory!

Meanwhile, Miltiades' wife helped him prepare for battle.

Defeating the Persians will not be easy, Hegesipyle. We both know what great fighters they are.

Miltiades had once been in the Persian army. But he and King Darius were now *mortal* enemies.

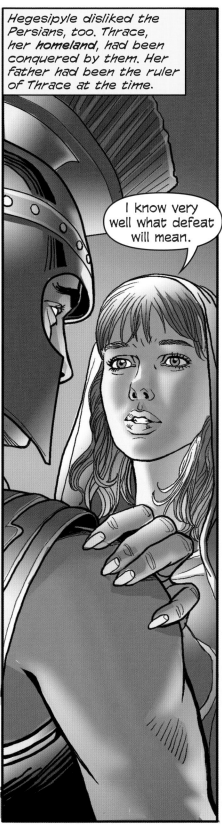

Hegesipyle disliked the Persians, too. Thrace, her *homeland*, had been conquered by them. Her father had been the ruler of Thrace at the time.

I know very well what defeat will mean.

I will not let the Persians reach the gates of Athens!

The Persians will not expect you to attack with a smaller force. Use surprise to your *advantage*.

If only women were allowed to fight. Then I would have my revenge, too!

11

13

The next morning, the Athenian soldiers prepared for battle.

Are you sure you're okay to fight? You've run so far these past few days.

I am ready. Which group are you in?

I'm on the right. My brother is in the center group. He'll get all the *glory.*

Does Aeschylus realize the danger his brother faces? The center group may not survive this battle.

CHARGE!

Miltiades' tactic worked. The Persians were taken by surprise. The center group of Athenians charged. The speed of the attack gave the Persian archers little time to shoot their arrows.

Soon, the Persians stopped the Athenians' center attack. Then, the two other Athenian forces closed in from the sides.

After several hours of fighting, the Persians realized they were beaten. They fled to their ships. The Athenians followed them.

The Persians lost thousands of men. The Greeks lost only 192. Callimachus died a hero.

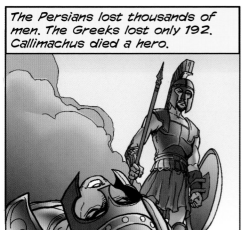

So did the brother of Aeschylus.

You died fighting for Athens. My plays will record your glory.

Aeschylus, soon you will have time to *grieve*. But now we must return to Athens.

The Persians are sailing for our city. They know that we are all here. Athens is *defenseless!* We must get there first.

19

The Athenian soldiers rapidly marched back to Athens.

When the Persian leaders saw the Greek soldiers ready to fight again, they decided to sail away for home.

For Athens, and its citizens, the victory was complete.

Phidippides is still remembered for his sacrifice. Today, long-distance foot races are called marathons. They honor Phidippides' heroic run.

Wrap Up

At Marathon, tiny Athens defeated the great army of Darius. Afterward, Athens became the leading city-state of Greece. Years later, the son of Darius sent a huge army back to Greece. He wanted revenge. I wrote about that war, too.

In this story, we saw some of the tension between Athens and Sparta. These Greek powers were often in conflict. Every four years, though, all the city-states stopped fighting during the Olympic Games. Sports brought different cultures together. This is still true today.

Read more about the Olympics in *The Modern Olympics: Battling for Peace.*

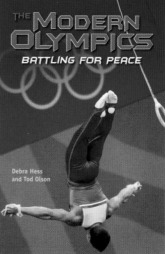

THE MODERN OLYMPICS
BATTLING FOR PEACE

Debra Hess and Tod Olson

Glossary

advantage (*noun*) something that may help you to do better

ally (*noun*) a country that has an agreement to support another country

ambush (*verb*) to attack someone from a hiding place

charge (*noun*) a rush forward to attack

conquer (*verb*) to defeat an enemy; to take over a place by force

defeat (*verb*) to win a victory over a competitor

defenseless (*adjective*) without protection; vulnerable

forum (*noun*) a public place where debates are held

glory (*noun*) great fame or honor that comes from doing something important

grieve (*verb*) to feel great sadness, especially at a death or loss of something

homeland (*noun*) the country where someone was born

might (*noun*) great power or strength

mission (*noun*) an important task

mortal (*adjective*) very hostile or intense

opposition (*noun*) a group or attitude that fights against another group or idea

playwright (*noun*) someone who writes plays

sequence (*noun*) a set of things in a particular order

tactic (*noun*) a method or plan used to achieve a goal

terrain (*noun*) a type of land

Idioms

go to great lengths (*page 2*) to try very hard
We will go to great lengths to win the game.

won't let them down (*page 7*) you won't be disappointed
Our social studies project won't let them down.